SPIRITUAL ANTENNA

By Shirley Blackwood

Poetry

Copyright © 2019: Shirley Blackwood

All rights reserved. No part of this publication may be produced, distributed, or transmitted in any form or by any means, including photocopying, recording, or other electronic or mechanical methods, without the prior written permission of the publisher, except in the case of brief quotations embodied in critical reviews and certain other non-commercial uses permitted by copyright law.

First Printed in United Kingdom 2019

Published by Conscious Dreams Publishing
www.consciousdreamspublishing.com

ISBN: 978-1-912551-66-8

DEDICATION

To those who are feeling alone and brokenhearted.

ACKNOWLEDGEMENTS

First of all, I would like to thank the Almighty God for giving me the ability to write. All glory and honour goes to Him!

I would like to thank my husband Floyd, my daughters Chantel, Stephanie, Sherene, my nephew Desmond, my Mother, and my sister Sandra.

My gratitude also goes to Pastor Richard Marzetti and my 'family' at Chatsworth Baptist Church for giving me a platform to share my poems during the service.

Rachel and Duncan thank for the support and encouragement.

My dearest friend Stephanie George, many, many, thanks for your prayers and support.

To Daniella Blechner at Conscious Dreams Publishing for making my poetical aspirations come true. Thank you also to Oksana Kosovan who typeset my beautiful book. Thank you to those who are too many to mention for believing in me.

MESSAGE FROM THE AUTHOR

I love nature and being aware of the beauty presented around me. I have a passion for gardening and singing. I am a member of the Praise and Worship Team at my church and in a local Community Choir.

I started writing poetry as a teenager as a means of getting in touch with my emotions in a deep and spiritual way. Although I was not aware of it at the time, when I looked back, I realised that my poems were being used to speak to the hearts of the vulnerable and broken hearted.

There are so many people who are in need of finding release to their deep rooted pain and SPIRITUAL ANTENNA will help them connect to what cannot be verbally expressed. I hope this collection of my poems will assist those in need of receiving healing and restoration.

CONTENTS

Dry My Tears 11

God, Is That You Calling? 13

Teach Me to Trust 14

Pain 15

Hope 17

The Cross 18

Our Light 19

Always and Forever 20

Moment of Love 21

She Is Beautiful 22

Ladies 23

Spring 24

Little Eden 25

Greed 26

Unlock Your Giving Door 27

He Put Me Back Together 28

Hear My Cry 29

My Husband 30

Release 31

Hopeless Endeavour to Make Us Fall	32
Who the Cap Fits	33
He Told Me He Loved Me	35
Such Love	36
All For Love	37
Stressed	38
Why?	39
Villain or Victim	40
Gifts	42
The Fire Is Burning	43
Christ Is Born	44
Worship Only You	45
Hold on	46

Dry My Tears

My soul cries
My heart cries
My spirit cries
We are all crying

I have suffered
I am not innocent
I have messed up
I have had my cup

Dry my tears
Mend my heart
Heal my spirit
Give me a new start
Oh, how I've cried, deep from my soul
Only you know how I've felt, my soul
I have been crying for many years
The problem is no one saw my tears
But you, oh Lord, have always been there
Take me to that level that I have tried so long to reach
I am at your door,

Knocking, to find your peace
Am I angry with you Lord?
Yes, I am
Please forgive me, as I am trying to understand
That in my brokenness, you are my
guiding hands

God, Is That You Calling?

God is that you calling?
Is that your voice I hear?
Are you trying to gain my attention?
To tell me that you care?

God, you know I am hurting
Saddened by grief
Death came and snatched her away
Just like a thief

God, I am falling
I know you understand
I feel so helpless
I am a broken man

God, please forgive me
The times I fail to hear
But when death came and broke my world
It left me in despair

Teach Me to Trust

Teach me to trust in your wonderful name
Knowing that hope in you is for certain
Uplift me when I am feeling down
Please don't let me bear this pain alone

I know you promise to be right by my side
But sometimes Lord, I just want to hide
Away from the torture, I feel within

But I know you understand as you see
deep within
Give me a new beginning
Lord, let me stand
Forever, by your guided hands

Pain

My heart cries the bitter tears of pain
Even my soul is in ruins
Where can I go, Where can I hide?
From this feeling I have inside

If I was beaten, black and blue
I would cry please let these pains be true
Because they are for just a while
But the pain of heartache is like losing a child

Where can I go?
Where can I hide?
From this hurt I have inside
For one day, my heart may be well
How will I know, how will I tell
To love you so much
It's hard to explain
Why I ask myself, have you caused me this pain?
Was I not good enough for you?
You took my heart and were untrue

For sadness does not only occur when a person dies
Sadness exists within my eyes
Look closer and you will see
The sadness that dwells inside of me

Hope

Never give up trying
Even when times are tough
Though you hear yourself say
I have had enough

Never give up hoping
That your dreams will come true
Hope is what you should look for
As hope looks out for you

Hope wants you to plan
To see your future from afar
Hope lights up your world
Like a shining star

Hope is relying on what you do not see
And when you put your trust in hope
It becomes reality

The Cross

It is finished, it is done
The cross took our pain
It claimed the life of God's only son
Who had no sin or shame
He took all our sufferings
In drops of sweat – like blood
They could not stay awake with him
They never understood

The agony that awaited him
No one could ever bear
As he was the chosen one
To show the world he cared

He took with him our suffering
He took with him our pain
But on that very third day
His victory we have gained

Our Light

Our light is still shining
Many years on
It hasn't always been easy to keep our lights on
We have struggled to keep them alight
But the Lord has always been with us
To keep our lights shining bright

So let us all remember
That His will, will be done
And to put our trust in him
Father, spirit and son

Let our lights illuminate
For all the world to see
The beauty of the Lord
That attracted you and me

Keep them beaming
Never let them go dim
Children of God
Continue to seek the light in him

Always and Forever

Always and forever
That is our predestined vow
To share our lives together
In whatever life bestows

And when the times are shaky
And the future may seem dim
We'll go on our knees in prayer
And let Christ enter in

For we are meant for each other
This is a part of our call
No matter what happens
Love will conquer all

Moment of Love

Come kiss my lips, designed for you
Wrap your arms around me
Embrace me, feel my hot breath
Touch me with your trembling caress
Let our souls melt in this moment of love

She Is Beautiful

She is beautiful
A gift from God above
Her eyes are like an angel
Face of purest love

She is our beautiful daughter
God gave to you and me
She's a part of God's love
For all of the world to see

Ladies

Ladies, it's your time to listen
To hear from the royal throne
You are fearfully and wonderfully made
In the image of God alone
Give yourselves credit
For what you have achieved
A parent or non-parent, you have all lived

You are charming, wonderful beings
Adorable in the eyes of God
Relax in your domain
Shake off the stress
No matter what you've experienced
You are eternally blessed

Spring

Daffodils are blooming
Spring is on its way
The colours are alluring
We are in for brighter days
Tulips are up and coming
The birds happily sing their songs
The door is closed on a season
As we welcome another one

Little Eden

Little Eden, blackened by clouds of darkness
Shadows of trees under the darkened covering
Fences, tables and chairs just mere shapes
Aroma of flowers dominates the air
Interlocked within the darkness
Little Eden, hides its beauty in homage to God

Greed

Horatio my love
Why did you displease me?
Why did you lie to Antonio?
For he was your brother
Who sacrificed his life for your freedom
Was money so precious
That you sold your soul
And denied your own brother his life?
Oh poor wretched Horatio my love
Life was once so beautiful with you by my side
You have changed Horatio
You have cheated and lied

Unlock Your Giving Door

There are those who are poor and hungry
Whose needs are to receive
Let's give in helping
To satisfy their needs

Be an example of Jesus
Who always helped the poor
Don't close your heart to giving
Unlock your giving door

For when you were broken
And thought that all was lost
Christ gave himself for you
As a ransom on the cross

Be a beacon in giving
Be a beam of light
For giving is love in action
Illuminating the world with God's light

He Put Me Back Together

I heard about this man Jesus
That he was passing by
That he healed people
Such as you and I
That he made the lame walk
And the blind to see
And his arms are always open
For people like you and me

He put me back together
He bound up my wounds
He carried me like a father
In all I was going through

Hear My Cry

Lord of host
Please hear my plea
As I am calling out to thee

Hear my cry
I know you understand my pain
As my heart is raining once again

I long so much to be set free
To walk with you in my company
To hold your hand, to feel safe
To trust in your amazing grace

Lord, I cannot express how I feel
But you know my pain is real
Don't let me bear this pain alone
Please walk with me from now on

My Husband

He was my husband
My one true friend
He was my soul mate
I loved him till the end

When sickness stepped in
My future seemed dim
But yet I had faith as I knew that God
was with him

In his suffering he never denied
That he'll meet with the saviour on the
other side

His faith was strong
Stronger than mine
But now he's gone and I'm left behind
But I thank God for the times we had
Although in my heart I'm still feeling sad

Release

Unveil my heart
Expose my mind
To the hidden talents that are inside me
Hope is my strength and is prolonged
It gives me energy
Yes, it makes me strong

My soul awakens, I do see
The beauty that God has placed in me
For there was a time, I could not see
As fear had gripped me completely

Afraid to speak
Afraid to stand
Afraid to ask for a helping hand

My heart unveiled
My mind at peace
God has given me release
From the prison of fear and pain
As I continue to call on his name

Hopeless Endeavour to Make Us Fall

So you are trying to make us fall
No you won't we'll always stand tall
So you're trying to make us give in
No we'll never give in to sin
So you're trying to run us down
No you can't for God's kingdom is
about to come

So you're trying to make us blind
No you can't because he will save mankind
So you think it will be fun
To hit us hard to make us run
Oh poor wretched fool you are
You have gone way too far

Who the Cap Fits

What is your purpose?
What is your game?
For money, are you willing to send your brother insane?

What is your destiny?
Do you have hope?
Are you happy, to slowly kill your brother, by selling him dope?

What is your reason?
For selling crack cocaine, heroin or hash
To the children
Your tormented mind is only on cash

But one day,
You'll surely be caught
For the lives you have taken
For the tears you have brought

For the suffering you have caused
For the heartless decisions you have made
Your time is running out
You'll certainly be paid

To those who help the pushers supply,
You think you are innocent that this
doesn't apply
But check yourself – revisit your mind,
Stop helping the pushers, stop being so blind

He Told Me He Loved Me

He told me how much he loved me
And took my heavy load
He mended my broken spirit
Deep within my soul
He promised never to leave me
That he'd be by my side
That he is my father
Protector and my guide

Such Love

I never knew such love
As your love for me
You gave it all at Calvary to set me free

You listened to my problems
You understood my pain
You promised me a brand new future
That my life will never be the same
Such wonderful love
No other can bring
As the blood you shed for me
That paid for all my sins

All For Love

Father in heaven
Your love is divine
You gave your son to save mankind
To secure a place for each of us
All you ask of us is to believe and trust
In your words and by faith
By demonstrating love and living by grace
By helping each other in moments of need
It was for this you sacrificed your only seed

Stressed

My body is pressed and my mind is a strain
My head is heavy
Who understands my pain?
My strength is depleted
Sleep is but a surface thing
Not a deep release as normal
My body is wrecked
There is tension in my neck
Who can feel my pain?

Who understands or hears my cry?
Who can feel my pain?
Who understands my pressured sigh?
Who can feel my pain?
Do you see me, the whole of me?
Or do you see what you want?
Do you hear my cry for relief?
Who can feel my pain?

Why?

Is it the colour of my skin that offends you?
Do I belong ?
Am I recognised?
Why am I always overlooked?
Are you so blind?
Don't you realise that I too belong to the family
of mankind?
Yes, my colour is black
Well does that mean that I should be
an outcast?
I need to be seen
And to be treated like a human being

Villain or Victim

The train is packed
I've got to get on
There are so many people standing on
the platform
I cannot be late for a second time
I've got to get to work, don't want to be
left behind

Yes it's late once again
But who's to blame for this shame?
The crowd move forward and I with them
A shove from behind and I am in

Accidentally I stepped on his toes
Sorry I said but he attacked me with blows
I tried so hard to explain
But for a few minutes the man had gone insane

As I shrivelled in fear
The carriage was packed but no one
seemed to care
It's not my business someone said
Though blood was running from my head

Leave her alone another voice said
Can't you see she's bleeding from her head?
She was only trying to get on the train
And someone shoved her forward she's
not to blame
To which of you does this apply?
Are you the villain or the victim?

Gifts

Perhaps you have a gift to sing
Praises to our God and king
Maybe you are a preacher man
Who leads his flock to follow God's plan

Could you be the one who prophesies?
Who hears the voice of God on high
Or are you financially blessed
Who shares with those who do not possess

You may be that listening ear
Who gives up your time to show that you care
Perhaps you are that very one
Who comforts those feeling down

No matter what your gift may be
Remember they are only temporary
Use them in the best way that you can
To honour the name of Christ – God's son

The Fire Is Burning

The fire is burning
It's burning bright
The angels are singing
The bells are ringing
The star brings forth
It's celestial light

The babe in a manger
In the stable of strangers
The wise men bring their gifts
They behold the glory
To tell their story
Of the Christ
The new born king

Christ Is Born

Holy, holy stars shining bright
Look upon this wonderful sight
As angels sing their melodious songs
In welcome of the holy lamb
Can you hear the heavenly sound?
Can you hear it? It's all around
The bells are ringing
Hallelujah they sing
Christ is born our heavenly king

Worship Only You

My life is to worship
Jesus Christ the king
Whose blood was shed to wash away my sins
So how can I deny
What I'm called to do?
I surrender my life
To worship only you

Hold on

When your heart is breaking
And you feel you can't go on
When you feel you've been trying
But everything seems to go wrong
When you are at the edge of surrendering
to your pain
Don't give up, as your testing is not in vain

Hold on for tomorrow will be another day
Where hopes and dreams are renewed
And tears are washed away
Hold on to God's promise
As He will see you through
He hasn't forgotten
As He is holding on to you

www.ingramcontent.com/pod-product-compliance
Lightning Source LLC
Chambersburg PA
CBHW021126080526
44587CB00010B/644